REJOICE

and

BE GLAD!

(Y)OURS IS THE KINGDOM OF GOD

DAVID HAAS

WITH ORIGINAL ART BY

BROTHER MICKEY

clear *faith*
PUBLISHING

Published by Clear Faith Publishing, LLC
781 Caxambas Drive
Marco Island, FL 34145
www.clearfaithpublishing.com

All acknowledgements of quotes from musical selections can be found on page 107

Also available: Rejoice and Be Glad: {Y}Ours is the Kingdom of God (CD-1058)
CD and individual music editions, from GIA Publications, Inc. 7404 South Mason
Avenue, Chicago, IL 60638 www.giamusic.com

Original art: Bro. Mickey McGrath, OSFS

Cover and interior design: Doug Cordes

Author photo: Helen Haas

ISBN: 978-1-940414-27-0

The mission of Clear Faith Publishing is to spread joy, peace, and comfort through
great writing about spirituality, religion, and faith that touches the reader and serves
those who live on the margins. Portions of the proceeds from our Homilists for the
Homeless series are donated to organizations that feed, shelter, and provide counsel
for those in need. For more information please visit us at www.clearfaithpublishing.com

TO JIM WALDO,

for his friendship and for suggesting

the F minor chord.

Contents

Through the lens of his justly popular song-prayer "Blest Are They" (one of my all-time favorites), David Haas, one of the church's greatest liturgical musicians, has provided us fresh thinking and challenging words to invite us to a passionate commitment to live the Beatitudes. But these are not gentle and soothing words. Instead, readers will discover a heart-stirring and spirit-filled framework to follow Christ in brand new ways. Read this book to live, pray, serve—and, of course, sing!—as if for the very first time.

JAMES MARTIN, SJ
Author of *Jesus: A Pilgrimage* and *The Jesuit Guide*

David Haas' prayerful reflections on the ancient Beatitudes [Matthew's version] sing in many ways. They take on the communal nature of songs, commands, reminders, encouragement, and blessings. The text is interspersed with lyrics of his own songs and others, and from the text of Pope Francis' *Gaudete et Exsultate*, calling us to make the words and the hopes of Jesus come true in reality today in our lives and in our world. In the gospel's familiar words, in the Pope's more contemporary suggestions and in the musical expressions, Jesus' blessings on those who are favored to enter and live in his dwelling among us now on earth are celebrated. And even more so, we are invited once again to come, encourage one another and to draw others into God's place of refuge now. And we are invited to come singing, drawing others into Francis of Assisi's merry band of troubadours; psalm singers and holy fools seeking to live God's Good News to the Poor.

MEGAN MCKENNA
Theologian and author

Rejoice and Be Glad reveals the heart behind the song that we often sing in liturgical settings. David Haas speaks of his own exploration of the Beatitudes in everyday living. This work extends Pope Francis' exhortation into the American faith experience. Best of all for me, though, was it made a treasured hymn live in a new way through the experience of the artist...a joy to be recommended.

SR. SIMONE CAMPBELL, SSS
Executive Director, Network Lobby for Catholic Social Justice

David Haas, that wonderful songwriter and musician, has crafted a rich symphony, weaving song and reflection through the lens of 'Blest Are They.' He invites us to journey into the heart of Jesus' message voiced in the Beatitudes and take on a new way of living a radical Christian life. It is a clear call to be attentive and intentional when we lift our hearts in song and sing, 'Blest Are They,' who build bridges instead of walls, who advocate for the immigrant and the voiceless, and lift people from fear and shame. Each chapter helps us to choose new paths that will bring spiritual freedom and transformation of mind and heart. This book is a 'must read 'and wonderful guide for anyone who wishes to deepen their relationship with Jesus and live a life of blessedness and happiness in today's world.

EDITH PRENDERGAST, RSC
Former Diocesan Director of Religious Education
Archdiocese of Los Angeles

Blest are they, the poor in spirit, theirs is the
kingdom of God.
Blest are they, full of sorrow, they shall be consoled.
Blest are they the lowly ones, they shall inherit
the earth.
Blest are they who hunger and thirst, they shall have
their fill.
Blest are they who show mercy, mercy shall be theirs.
Blest are they, the pure of heart, they shall see God.
Blest are they who seek peace, they are the children
of God.
Blest are they who suffer in faith, the glory of
God is theirs.
Blest are you who suffer hate, all because of me.
Rejoice and be glad, yours is the kingdom, shine for
all to see!
Rejoice and be glad!
Blessed are you, holy are you!
Rejoice and be glad!
Yours is the kingdom of God!

Introduction

> "Can anything good come from Nazareth?"
>
> **(JOHN 1: 46)**

I need to begin
by telling you that I

actually began work on this book two months before Pope Francis released his apostolic exhortation, *Gaudete et Exsultate* ("Rejoice and be Glad"). Honest to God. However, after realizing this, I thought I should stop working on this project when the exhortation was published, but my friends Jim Knipper and Fr. James Martin, SJ, told me to keep moving forward. Jim Martin had only one challenge, "Just be sure that this will speak to our faith."

In all honesty, when I composed the song "Blest are They" in 1984, I really did not have any deep understanding of how critical the Sermon on the Mount, and in particular, its beginning verses that make up the Beatitudes, truly is in terms of what it means to follow Jesus.

It was six years after I had left Bridgeport, Michigan, and had moved to St. Paul, Minnesota. After completing my seminary studies (where I discerned that priesthood was not my vocation), and having served only three years in parish ministry, I was in more ways than not, a true novice. I was only twenty-five at the time of the song's creation. I just had not lived enough life yet. Now, I had certainly always admired the attributes of what Jesus was teaching in the Sermon on the Mount. I had also always believed that the Beatitudes provided a blueprint of how I was supposed to live my life, and how we as a people, the Body of Christ, were to behave.

The song "Blest Are They" originally sprung forth from a place of gratitude, which certainly is a good grounding to have when creating anything, especially when it comes to sung prayer. At the time of its writing I was not planning or setting out to compose a musical setting of the Beatitudes. Up to this point these verses seemed very intimidating to me, and so it was not on my radar screen as a composer. It was composed while I was director of liturgy and music at St. Thomas Aquinas parish in St. Paul Park, Minnesota (1982-1985), and when I was part of the volunteer team that participated in the "Loaves and Fishes" program that was established at the Dorothy Day Center in St. Paul. Once or twice a month we would prepare and serve a meal to the homeless and other "guests" (as Dorothy would always call them) who would arrive for dinner. My friend Barbara Colliander was the coordinator for our team, and while observing her manner of attentiveness to the broken and destitute who showed up that very first time I volunteered, I was deeply moved and discovered a profound and teachable witness that we are each called to exhibit in our care, hospitality, generosity, and honoring of all people. With

Dorothy Day as her model, my friend Barbara was able to see and celebrate the holiness that streams forth from the most unlikely vessels—in this case, the poor ones, the "least of these" that Jesus was always so concerned about. I was humbled by what I saw in Barbara's loving presence and attentiveness to each and every person who came through those doors.

While driving home after that first night of this profound experience, all I could think of was how through her eyes and by her being present Barbara was saying to each of these wonderful saints of God: "Blessed are you! Holy are you!" When I finally got home, the Beatitudes became my guide for this song that I composed in about ten minutes. I could not scribble the notes and words down fast enough—I was compelled, one could say. But more so, I felt thankful. It was not created because of any pure musical or compositional skill, but primarily as I have said, from a place of deep gratitude.

That was 1984, and there are so many stories and memories of this song that have flowed forth since then. At the time of its writing, I could have never predicted the eventual popularity of the song—that has led it to being the number one biggest "seller" among all of my liturgical compositions and among the same for the entire catalog of music from my publisher, GIA Publications in Chicago. Over the years it has appeared in numerous hymnals of diverse Christian denominations throughout the world and has been translated into countless languages. It was sung in the presence of Saint Pope John Paul II on September 16, 1987 at the papal mass at Dodger Stadium in Los Angeles and there are literally hundreds of "covers" of the song, appearing on various CD recordings and You-Tube videos. Alongside my song "You Are Mine," it is the song that I am thanked for the most among people I meet, who often have their own stories to share about how the song has touched their lives. For me personally, my most cherished memories of "Blest Are They" are the times when I have been able to lead people in the singing of it at the site of Israel's Mount of Beatitudes while leading pilgrimages there. Still, regardless of the song's setting or occasion, I still think of that evening at the Dorothy Day Center every time I sing it.

But as thirty-five years have passed since its creation, my understanding of the implications of the Sermon on the Mount have expanded and I have been feeling the ground beneath my feet shake more and more every time I sing this song-prayer. Pope Francis, in *Gaudete et Exsultate*, has also shaken up my heart a hundred-fold with a renewed sense of enlightened wisdom and offers a challenge for all Christians.

Certainly, I still hold on to, and still celebrate, the story and journey that the song has taken in my own spiritual life and for the prayer lives of those who have sung and prayed it over the years. But I am being taken deeper into the mystery of the Beatitudes and what they still continue to teach as I explore my own vocation as a disciple of Jesus. Through deeper study and reading the insights of people like N.T. Wright, Fr. Michael Crosby, OFM Cap; Fr. John Dear, Nadia Bolz-Weber, and my dear friends Art Zannoni, Fr. Michael Joncas, and Fr. Richard Rohr, OFM, and through taking more time in prayer around this sermon, I am coming to see more clearly my belief in what the Beatitudes are intended to be, through the eyes of Christ, and less of what they have been, viewed through my imperfect lens as a sinner.

I am learning that the Beatitudes are *not* a "self-help" book on how we are to live as Christians. I am learning that it is shallow to reduce these verses to being a "rule book" or "curriculum" for how to get into heaven. But they most certainly are a reflection of Jesus' mission and invitation to embrace a more "downward mobility"—for us to take the baton from him to be a "kingdom people," committed servants consumed with being wrapped in the reign of God. They are not a template for how we are to behave. They are, more accurately, about who Jesus really is, and how *he* rules.

Jesus aches to have this reign come to life in the world through the sorts of people described in these verses—people like himself. People like us. The Sermon on the Mount is a call for us to take up our vocation to be light and life for the world, and to show the world what this reign of God looks like. It is a call (please pardon the crude imagery) to spit upon the values and the secular "religion" of our culture so often embodied in this world. Jesus not only promoted downward mobility, but even more prophetically, he witnessed a downward *nobility*. He certainly did just that when he chose to mount an emaciated donkey on his entrance into Jerusalem—intentionally mocking the emperor triumphantly entering the square on a majestic white horse. His entire life was preaching and *living* the Beatitudes, in direct defiance of the state, society, and the norms of his time. I am more and more convinced that the Sermon on the Mount, and particularly the Beatitudes, is a clarion call to put on the cloak of that same defiance.

Every time we sing "Blest are..." we need to be tethered

to both the Hebrew and Greek understanding of "bless," which means to be "set aside" or apart for a specific purpose. When applied to God it means that God is setting a person apart from the regular, and in service of the divine or the "holy." When Jesus preaches the Beatitudes he is challenging us to recognize that God has "set us apart" from the sacred in order to purvey the holy to humankind. To be baptized into becoming a "Sermon on the Mount People" is to abandon the family of our origin and take on the family of *choice*—the Jesus family. Jesus makes this clear in response to the woman who cries out, "Blessed is the womb that bore you and the breasts that nursed you!" Jesus, the teacher, counters her claim by asserting, "Blessed rather are those who hear the word of God and obey it!" (Luke 11:27-28)

The Beatitudes offer us a concrete examination of conscience. Singing and praying "Blest are They" has, in recent years, been the seed of such an examination for me even though it was composed many years ago. It is continually becoming an act of confession and commitment for me to announce a new understanding of Easter that I have never considered before: this song-prayer is a charge to proclaim that God's way is not the way of the world; to change the world, we have to think and act in radically non-judgmental and nonviolent ways. To change this world, God chooses not to cast anyone away, so to announce that this love is to be shared lavishly, as the Sisters of St. Joseph of Carondelet would assert "without distinction." To change the world, God's way is not to have the tanks roll in or utilize weapons to dominate under the banner of fear with an arsenal of pure might. God does not send people into the line of fire to keep the peace, but, rather, God calls servants and disciples to *be the peace*. The peace of God is not found through sheer will and incitement through threat, and does not exhibit strength through the building of walls or the building up of instruments of so-called "deterrence," but through the presence of vulnerability, trust, and reconciliation.

God does not send in authorities to judge and condemn, and does not send in the armies. No, God sends into this world the meek, the sad and mourning, the broken, those who ache for justice, the peacemakers and the ones brimming with mercy, those who know deep suffering from living at the margins, and those who are mocked for doing so. This is God's way—God's unique pedagogy of downward mobility. What are the attributes, attitudes, and qualities of this journey? Generosity, forgiveness, mercy, and restorative justice. This is God's true peace.

To follow in God's way is not to adhere to rules that will manipulate us in any way to behave better. What God wants from us is for us to "rejoice and be glad," and to do so in the midst of this alternative yet beautiful—and much more effective *and* affective in the end—path that leads us to choose differently than we presently do in this world. We are to do more than sign up for a program that's reduced to outlining a code of ethics, pushing us into keeping certain practices (that often are, albeit, worthy practices). The Beatitudes are an *announcement*, a trumpet blast calling us each to conversion toward a radical change of life, to take on new ways of doing things and new ways of living our lives.

What are the specifics of this "new way?" The path is one where we courageously accept and bring to heel policies and initiatives that keep people in bondage; that keep people trapped in poverty and exclusion. We are to push, prod, and provoke systems that refuse to forgive debt that strangles the quality of life for the poor, the hungry, and the homeless. It means not tolerating economic conditions that allow the poor to become poorer, without a home, without food, and without dignity.

The new way of the Beatitudes calls for us to protect our planet; to build bridges instead of walls; to advocate for the weak and voiceless; to banish all discrimination and dynamics that may separate us; to lift people from shame and isolation who are put there because of their sexual orientation and their choice of who to love; and to reject any form of violence—period. To take on this way of living means that we cannot tolerate or withstand the absence of peace because to not be ambassadors of peace is to not live in right relationship with God. The absence of peace is anti-Easter and anti-Gospel.

This new way is to *shout*—and *sing*—as loud as we can, in order to reach as many who will hear the truth and good news that God is real; God weeps when we weep and rejoices when we rejoice. The scope and sequence of the Sermon on the Mount helps to break open all of the other great proclamations and songs of our biblical mandate: where the *Magnificat* (Luke 1: 46-55) becomes our anthem, holding the promise of the humble and meek toppling the decimation brought about by the mighty, and the thrones upon which they sit. The Beatitudes illustrate more than any other source "What would Jesus do?" by exposing what Jesus actually *did*. Jesus fed the hungry. Jesus healed the sick. Jesus sought after and collected his sheep and brought them close to his side. Jesus confronted the systems that threatened the lives of people. Jesus refused to tolerate the situation of his day that led to discrimination and isolation of people who society deemed unacceptable. Jesus offered us a peace that the "world cannot give" (John 14:27), but with the mandate that we are to be God's apprentices and spread such peace into the hearts of all people.

If we are to take them seriously, the Beatitudes should take our breath away with the enormity of its mandate. And, yes, from its sometimes-shallow foundation, build a new church that actually has, in many ways, become complicit (whether consciously or subconsciously) in keeping the status quo, which actually works against being the Body of Christ. The Beatitudes are teaching us (because we still have not really gotten it yet) that we are to continue this mission of Jesus. This is what Paul means when he instructs us to "put on Christ" (Galatians 3:27). Following Jesus is not about *going* to church; it is about *becoming* Church. It is not about being born again—it is about being born again *and again and again and again*.

I think the same is true for the song and me. I sing it so often, at just about every event—whether it be a concert, workshop, or retreat—that I think I sometimes forget about being born again and again each time I sing it. When I am honest with myself, I sometimes zone out and forget about the biblical and musical examination of conscience that it really is. While I did *finish*, publish, and originally record the song many years ago, I have come to discover that it is far from being finished at all. I have discerned that I still have a lot of work to do with this song-prayer, and much more to learn in regards to what it is that I am announcing and giving witness to every time it is sung. This is the root of why I chose to write this book.

When the church teaches and embodies what Jesus is preaching and doing, it will most certainly provoke a response, just as Jesus received, that is not only filled with resistance, but at times with downright hostility. This is the path for those who embrace this most holy downward nobility: to take on the Beatitudes is to operate from the same stance that the early Church proclaimed as its self-identity in mission, articulated in the response that Peter and his band of followers announced while in the presence of the Sanhedrin: "Better for us to obey God than people!" (Acts 5:29). Peter must have known that saying and acting in such ways would result in punishment and yes, persecution. This is both the plight and *gift* for those of us who call ourselves Christian. It has always been so. There is no separation in the reign of God proclaimed in the Beatitudes and the eventual taking up of the cross. It is not only unavoidable, but it is inevitable—part of our "job description" of being what the early Church referred to as "followers of the way."

As is the case with many Catholic parish communities across the country and beyond, a dear friend of mine from the Diocese of Saginaw, Michigan (the diocese where I was born and grew up) was attending one of the meetings that her parish was holding (again, the parish where I was baptized and received my earliest formation in the faith along with my parents), to decide what the new name of the parish would be after they were informed that they were to cluster with two other parish communities in the area. She suggested not the name of one particular saint or figure, but rather, "The Church of the Beatitudes." Her suggestion did not get any traction at all. The thing is, when you name a community after a person or patron, they should try to embody the charism of that patron. Maybe being named as a community of "Beatitudes" was too daunting to even consider. Very understandable. Because it is, very daunting indeed. But to my thinking, my friend was tapping into some powerful wisdom of who saints really are—and the high calling that we are all invited to consider.

Now, this is heavy stuff. It might come off as being so lofty, so high-minded, so pure in its purpose—to numb us into believing that it is all just too impractical, too unattainable, too impossible. Some might say that it is naïve and out of touch with reality. Some may say, "Well, this is all well and good, but we have to deal with the *real* world." In other words, "David, just sing the nice song—don't preach."

The problem is that we have been getting it backwards for so long. It is Jesus' blueprint for the world that is to become the *most real*, and what we have come to know as every day is not *real* at all—it is deeply *false*. The mission is to reverse the tide and to make Jesus' reality—God's way—the norm. It is not to opt out, and say, "Well, all will be brought together in heaven." Jesus' mission—again, God's way—is a primal scream to our present way of doing things, that says "NO!" The Beatitudes are calling us to a new reformation, from supporting what I would call a "sweet and safe" Christianity, to embracing a most *dangerous* and *vulnerable* Christianity. When Jesus says, "My kingdom is not of this world" (John 18:36), our response should *not* be, "I wonder what Jesus meant by that?" Jesus *never* intended to bring about the reign of God alone. Jesus' mode of operation, his strategic plan was and is, always, that it be realized through human beings. He got this idea from God, as the "Bible tells us so."

God desires the world to be always oriented toward the poor and vulnerable, to the weak and isolated. And equally, as a result, God desperately wants people (that would mean you and me) to be responsible for this concern as a priority to be carried out. God wants and aches for peace. Again, equally, God wants the instruments of peacemaking to be you and me—God's daughters and sons. God passionately proclaims justice—not a punitive justice, but *restorative* justice, a justice that makes us each whole and complete. Once again, God's methodology for this justice is to send *us* to help the *false* world return to a most holy and *real* world. While I don't want to be judgmental (because I am at times a co-conspirator), when I lead "Blest are They" during concerts and other events and see people smiling and swaying back and forth, I wonder—do we really know what we are taking on here and giving our assent to while we are singing this? Maybe the melody is too lyrical, too pretty, too "upbeat." I guess what I am trying to say is that perhaps we need to be more intentional and attentive while we sing these words.

For the *Rite of Confirmation*, the refrain for one of the appointed responsorial psalms, Psalm 117, proclaims: "You will be my witnesses to all the earth" (Acts 1:8)—not to merely agree and give assent to God's vision for all creation—but to be purposed in mission; to step up and take on the "mantle of joy" that Isaiah proposes to us (Isaiah 61:3). It is my hope that this book—written through the lens of "Blest Are They" and adorned with the prophetic art of

Brother Mickey—might plant some seeds to help us delve into this profound undertaking that is encased in the mission of the Sermon on the Mount; to help us sing these most precious words as if it were the first time, and to send us forth into God's way and the path outlined by Jesus, our brother and deliverer. Then maybe, we will remember that we truly are blessed and holy; and that we can sing "rejoice and be glad" and really mean it and live it!

DAVID HAAS
THE SOLEMNITY OF ALL SAINTS
NOVEMBER 1, 2018

1

When JESUS *saw the* CROWDS...

The fifth chapter
of Matthew begins with,

what some might call, a prelude for the Beatitudes. But I believe it is more than that. It is the leitmotif through which we truly view not only the Beatitudes themselves, but the entire Sermon on the Mount. It shows us a Jesus who is *pastoral*, who knows how to "read the room," so to speak. He is responding to what is happening around him. And so, it begins:

"When Jesus saw the crowds…" (Mt. 5:1)

At this point, Jesus provides for us a corporate spirituality of the moment. It is not a personal introspection; it is a *communal* conversation. It is about *we*, not me. At the center of our vocation of being faithful to Jesus' teaching is the call to be a "Sermon on the Mount *People*." When he sees the crowds, he does not hesitate. He acts. Here Jesus is extending the covenant relationship that is established in the Hebrew Scriptures through the voice of the prophets. God is continually setting up this relationship with us, not in individual, specific relationships, but as a *people*: "I will be your God and you will be my people." We need to remember that at this time Jesus is taking on the task of reforming Judaism, moving it toward becoming a community of love, mercy, peace, and justice—not merely an organization strangled by the strict observance of laws and customs (believe it or not, establishing a new religion—namely Christianity—was *not* his goal). He is providing a model for all of us who serve in any corner of pastoral ministry to respond to the needs, cries, and aches of a *people*.

In the verses just before the beginning of this chapter, he offers this very formation for the first apostles: "Follow me, and I will make you fish for *people*" (Mt. 4:19b; emphasis mine), and then it immediately moves into specific concrete actions that serve to give public (not private) witness to God's presence among them: "Jesus went throughout Galilee, teaching in their synagogues and proclaiming the good news of the kingdom and curing every disease and every sickness among the *people*" (Mt. 4:23, emphasis mine). The result was that he attracted "great crowds" that "followed him from Galilee, the Decapolis, Jerusalem, Judea, and from beyond the Jordan" (Mt. 4:25). This teacher and healer responds to the needs and cries that are universal to all of us. Through his deeds and his greater mission, we are brought out of isolation and are tethered to one another as we search for a path to follow:

> God is ever wakeful, and always near:
> Watching, shielding, sheltering.
>
> **("GOD IS EVER WAKEFUL," BY DAVID HAAS)**

We are certainly not apathetic. We are, in fact, eager to not only hear but also to listen, although, ultimately, we do not know what will be asked of us.

Psalm 121 begins with a cry: "I lift my eyes to the mountains—from where will my help come?" (vs. 1). Mountains seem necessary for all of us seeking ongoing conversion in our lives; we talk about having profound spiritual encounters as being "mountain-top" experiences. Mountains are a big deal in the Bible, and anyone who has ever made a pilgrimage to the Holy Land understands this when visiting the holy sites, and realizes that so many of the events, stories, and settings happen on mountains: places like Mount Carmel, Mount Tabor, Masada, and yes the Mount of Beatitudes. The "mountain message" of the Beatitudes is what we need. We know from studying the Gospel of Matthew that his audience was primarily Jewish, and so for the author of Matthew, a key theme is to present Jesus as the "new Moses." As the Ten Commandments are the touchstones for a moral code in the Hebrew Scriptures, the nine Beatitudes become the clarity needed to move forward with this Jesus, in understanding both his humanity and his divinity. Mount Sinai and the commandments led people to the promised land. The Beatitudes, proclaimed on *this* mountain, proclaim and teach us who and what we are once we get there.

Jesus makes this concrete by going up on this mountain (Mt.5:b), then right away he "sits down" (which is a ritual direction from Judaism, for all to listen and be attentive to the "teacher")—and in that moment, the disciples come to him. The text does not tell us why. But we can infer that they recognize him as their teacher, and so, he begins to teach. He brings the "help" that has been the resounding cry of the nation for generations and generations. We, too, are one with Israel in our present time and situation. While the specific *content* changes with the various time periods and developments of history, the deeper truth remains eternal, grappling with the cries and struggles that have been the yearnings of the disciples and the crowd—are still true for us today. The basic cries of what it means to be human, as we try to navigate our way through both the joy and terror of life, always comes back to the same reality.

We are longingly in need of God. We are all looking for clarity. Even if we possess the greatest human versions of wisdom, in the end, we all seek some direction. We yearn for spiritual insight—that is why so many of us have spiritual directors; why we often make a retreat, or belong to a prayer or bible study group—because we want to understand, to be found, to be understood, to be seen, to believe that we matter and have worth. We are all looking for healing. We want to be and do good, but we fall short, and sometimes fail. Many of us want to be saints—but we also do not want to miss out on the lures and thrills of the world. So, like the crowd in this story we are seeking out Jesus, and we humbly approach the mountain in hope: "My help comes from the Lord, who made heaven and earth" (Psalm 121: 2). The beginning of the 12 steps of Alcoholics Anonymous teaches that we admit we are "powerless" and our lives have "become unmanageable." We come to "believe that a power greater than ourselves" can "restore us to sanity."

This is it, basically. We are looking for some sanity in the midst of all the insanity. We are in need of help. We are looking to find out what God's way *is*, and in Jesus, we begin to discover that way. We are looking up to the mountain. We are waiting for Jesus to speak.

2

BLEST

are they,

THE POOR IN SPIRIT...

theirs is the

KINGDOM OF GOD.

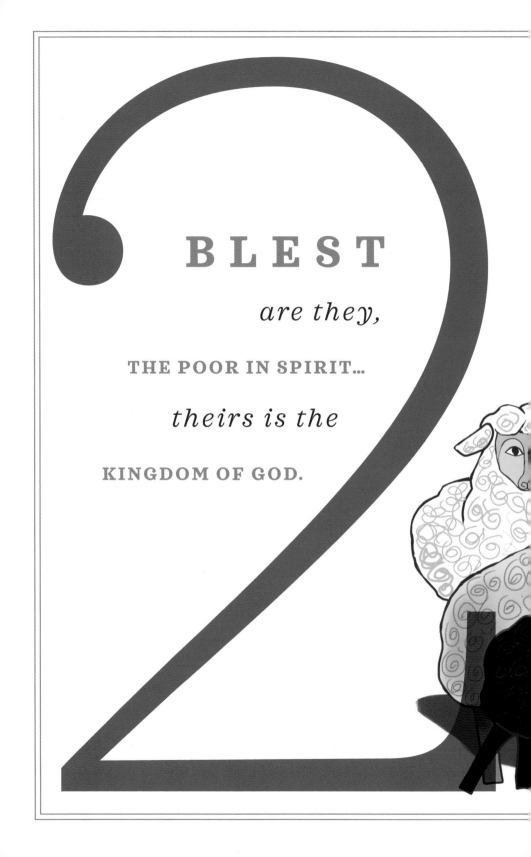

Each of the Beatitudes offers

a blessing to the believer and a renunciation to those agents, powers, and evils that stand in opposition to that blessing. The proclamation of this first Beatitude provides an unapologetic renunciation of all that is idolatrous. Money, greed, entitlement, domination, the gluttonous amassment of wealth for the sake of wealth—Jesus does not mince his words about these patterns, not only here in these verses but through the entirety of his teaching. Here is what Pope Francis has to say:

> The Gospel invites us to peer into the depths of our heart, to see where we find our security in life.
>
> Wealth ensures nothing. Indeed, once we think we are rich, we can become so self-satisfied that we leave no room for God's word, for the love of our brothers and sisters, or for the enjoyment of the most important things in life.
>
> In this way, we miss out on the greatest treasure of all. That is why Jesus calls blessed those who are poor in spirit, those who have a poor heart, for there the Lord can enter with his personal newness.

Being poor of heart: that is holiness.

(GAUDETE ET EXSULTATE, 67-68, 70)

Peter Maurin, co-founder of the Catholic Worker Movement with Dorothy Day, said it this way, cleverly expressed in one of his well-known "Easy Essays:"

The world would be better off,
if people tried to become better.
And people would become better
if they stopped trying to be better off.
For when everybody tries to be better off,
nobody is better off.
But when everybody tries to become better,
everybody is better off.

This first Beatitude challenges us all to "go back to school," and learn from the beginning what it means to follow Jesus. We are called to sell our material possessions as well as all of the trappings of power and elitism; all of the attributes that oppress and keep people down. This is a difficult call to hear and an even more difficult call to heed.

We are being invited to simply let go—of power, of status, of everything and anything that comes in the way of our right relationship with God. The poor understand this because in the midst of their poverty all they really have is their hope that God is with them; their steadfast belief is that they are not alone. Ironically, this provides many of them with an incredible sense of freedom, for often they can see and act clearly, without the distractions of the stuff that most of us can become so addicted to having. The poor, the "least of these," are broken. They have been knocked down time and again; by the standards of society they are powerless. But, by divine standards set much higher than those of secular society, they are wealthy beyond the human understanding of those of us who are more materially comfortable. The hope of the poor is neither a conviction nor certainty that poverty will be wiped away or that their condition will change. Their hope is found by knowing without a doubt that God is in the mix, and that they are not alone. Again, from Peter Maurin: "While modern society calls the beggars bums and panhandlers, they are, in fact, the Ambassadors of God."

I was talking to a group of people during a visit to the Philippines in the fall of 2016, and what I noticed was just how *happy* they all seemed to be. Many in this group were unemployed, poor, and living on the edge. Yet, they could not stop smiling! Their happiness was so infectious that I finally said to one of them: "You all seem so genuinely happy. Where does this come from? What is the source of your joy?" This lovely woman simply replied, "We just *choose* to be happy." My goodness, how pure and to the point! These people have made a *choice*. They seem to be able to make this choice because other things are not getting in the way of that choice. They have come to realize that they do not need many of the comforts which the rich have. They do not need much at all! They are unaware of where the next paycheck will come from, or if it will come at all. They are unable to know if they will be able to pay their bills, have their car fixed (if they have one to begin with), have the resources to visit the dentist, or repair the roof of their house. So, through the eyes of their faith and trust in God, they choose the only alternative—joy! A joy that celebrates that God *is*.

When we can free ourselves from the lure of having power or an exalted status in our communities—we can choose another way. We can see more clearly and act more assuredly with the surrender that God is asking of us. Let God be God. Be "poor" in the sense that, in the end, we really do not need anything else. Having possessions or a comfortable economic reality is not a sin in and of itself. But it can be the source of darkness if the desire for these possessions leads to a motivation directing *all* of our choices, including decisions and attitudes toward one another, or if it comes in the way of being transparent and vulnerable alongside our sisters and brothers in need. If our need for these worldly goods blocks our dependence on God and leads to an arrogance that provides false hope and preaches total self-sufficiency, then we are being called to participate in some self-reflection and perhaps some re-prioritization. If we are people who live more comfortably in the material way, then we are being invited to ask ourselves if these comforts in which we are surrounded have truly satisfied our needs, or if there is a deeper need not yet fulfilled. Let us allow the materially poor to teach us how we each are in desperate need of the deeper security that only God can provide. When we sing the beginning of this song, we need to remember this. May the sound that begins to come forth from our throat be wedded to a heart filled with surrender. May we see these beginning phrases as a celebration that the Beatitudes pull us toward coming closer to "the kingdom of God."

So, rejoice and be glad! Why? Because even in the darkest and most hopeless of times there really is nothing more that we need than for God to be by our side walking with us. Rejoice and be glad because with surrender comes freedom. Rejoice and be glad because our anxiety need not rule our hearts. In the end, while it may look differently for each of us, we are called to be poor. We are called to realize how desperately we need God. It is an invitation to celebrate and live intentionally, knowing the truth that it's the cross of Christ which dwells in our hearts and that God's grace is really, in the end, all that we need:

> The grace of God is all we need.
> Our strength is made perfect in our weakness.
> May we boast in the pow'r of Christ
> who dwells in us.
>
> **("IN THE POWER OF CHRIST," BY DAVID HAAS)**

The world says: How happy we are, and what a blessing it is to be comfortable, to have many possessions, property, and great success. Jesus says: How happy and blessed they are who have hit bottom, who have lost their spirit, for the reign of God belongs to them.

What do we say? How will we choose to live?

BLEST

are they,

FULL OF SORROW...

they shall

BE CONSOLED.

We all weep in one way or another.

I know I do. There are times, when for reasons I can't understand, I just feel sad. I just feel the need to cry. There are other times when I most assuredly *know* why I am sad, but that doesn't diminish the sting of the tears. We grieve things from our past or relive and nurture regrets as passionately as we recognize the pain caused by a fresh physical or emotional wound. The tears come, the chest tightens, the stomach churns, and the heart breaks once again. Sadness is just a part of being alive. Even in the situations where healing and restoration have taken place—the sadness still can come to us because our hearts actually feel attacked. So, yes, we need this Beatitude. Pope Francis can help all of us to understand this more deeply:

> The world has no desire to mourn; it would rather disregard painful situations, cover them up or hide them. Much energy is expended on fleeing from situations of suffering in the belief that reality can be concealed.
>
> But the cross can never be absent.
>
> A person who sees things as they truly are and sym-

pathizes with pain and sorrow is capable of touching life's depths and finding authentic happiness...Such persons are unafraid to share in the suffering of others; they do not flee from painful situations. They discover the meaning of life by coming to the aid of those who suffer, understanding their anguish and bringing relief.

They sense that the other is flesh of our flesh, and are not afraid to draw near, even to touch their wounds. They feel compassion for others in such a way that all distance vanishes.

Knowing how to mourn with others: that is holiness.

(GAUDETE ET EXSULTATE, 75-76)

This Beatitude of sadness and grief is the common experience of the entire population, of not only humanity but of Mother Earth, as well. However, like each of the Beatitudes, this sorrow provides an open door to God's heart; the generous heart of Jesus wants more than anything to embrace the struggle of sadness and grief so that we grow closer to God. To repeat Pope Francis' teaching, the "cross can never be absent." We know the many forms of sorrow that attack humanity; the infecting poison of discrimination; the conditions of extreme poverty; the violent pain that erupts from the horrors of war. There are so many more manifestations of sorrow where we simply find daily life too painful or filled with overwhelming grief and sadness. But we do not bear the pain alone.

Jesus does not walk away from our mourning and grieving; no, he leans closer into it, intentionally welcomes it in, and wears the sorrow just as we do. He walks with us. He does so with the crowd. For example, when Jesus sees the crowd their presence ignites the Sermon on the Mount. Of whom is this crowd comprised? People just like you and me—many who are on the outside of life and kept there by a society and structures of power that often provide nothing except discouragement and hopelessness. The "prosperity gospel" that infects our society tells us that there is no need to mourn, that it is through the misguided goals of financial security and "positive thinking" where we can find happiness, and that those who are able to attain it—*they* are the blessed ones. The crowd in the story also knows that the soldiers are just around the corner—and with that will come violence. Now, like then, we understand acts of war between nations because we face such violence, too. We also experience violence through the soldiers who enforce the desires of gun companies and political action groups to nurture violence in our own neighborhoods and schools— all for the sake of profit—an economic windfall achieved through the need to kill and destroy.

As we will hear about in chapter 8, you and I are called to be agents of peacemaking. Among the many costs involved in such a vocation is the *expectation* of sadness, grief, mourning, and lament. Yet, those who are full of sorrow are blessed by God. Jesus weeps over Jerusalem (Mt. 23:37-39 and Luke 19: 41-44) and in feeling the loss of his friend Lazarus (John 11:35). Can we find strength in knowing that God shares our sadness? Jesus certainly did as he walked directly into situation after situation of sadness. What was his response? His response was selfless compassion, not once, not twice, not sometimes. His response was selfless compassion *every single time*. His carrying the cross, literally as his own, is the great act of love and fidelity to each of us. Jesus shows us how God is feeling when sorrow seems to drench the earth. God is weeping. And God is anxious to provide comfort and reveal a most generous consolation.

Sorrow comes most of the time when we nurture our *amnesia* and *forget* that we are God's people. We are human beings, God's greatest creation—and we can be careless with this by either ignoring it, being indifferent to it, or turning our minds away from the circumstances of life that allow and encourage such sadness to inform our hearts. The result is that life seems for many to be a senseless exercise because there is such an absence of empathy and compassion or lack of sensitivity and attentiveness toward humanity. It should come as no surprise, then, that suicide is growing at an alarming rate in our world. If we can break through the systems and structures that are at the root of such violent sorrow—then we may be able to find recovery and remember that we are God's great, marvelous and wonderful *idea*. We are named as God's "work of art," or as another translation puts it, God's "great accomplishment" (Eph. 2:10).

We are brothers and sisters. Our Hawaiian friends name it *Ohana*, a family who shares in the "breath of life." In sharing this breath, no harm is allowed to be inflicted on one another because we are *Ohana* in the most intimate of relationships and in the splendor of all creation, on this earth and beyond. The challenge is that when we truly accept how tethered we are to one another, we have no other choice than to reject all the attitudes, policies, trends, and behaviors that are the root of our sorrow. We must *passionately* choose life and reject the forces that want to kill and destroy—regardless of the reason or any other "higher purpose." There can be no justification of violence if we look into the eyes, hearts, and lives of our sisters and brothers and name them to be children of God. It is impossible. It cannot be tolerated. We simply *do not kill*. We do not abuse or cause intentional harm. We are to offer only love. We are to be only agents and witnesses of compassion and peace. We are to join our sisters and brothers in their sorrow. The sorrow of others becomes our sorrow.

We are to be heralds of God's consolation. This Beatitude confronts us with the truth that there is no other life-response we can make if we claim Jesus as Lord. When we sing *this* verse of "Blest are They"—and when we sing the entirety of the song with integrity—let us not forget that the music of compassion is stronger than the death chant of spoken and harsh words—usually accompanied by actions—that only bring sadness to those who hear them.

Rejoice and be glad! Why? Because it *is* possible to expand our hearts. It is much more than possible because we see living signs of this from people who walk with the sorrowful, and who align themselves with the grief so deeply experienced in this world. God brings consolation and we see around and among us many people who have chosen this life in following Jesus. Rejoice and be glad because it is placed before us that other choices *can* be made besides the furthering of such sadness that drowns in sorrow. We *can* choose differently. We *can* walk with the sorrowful when we first come face to face with our own, and then move outside of ourselves in praying and singing a song that is relentless: "rejoice and be glad."

Why? Because consolation is *not* a false hope. Sorrow will always be with us. But the same is true in terms of how we reach out to such sorrow—and we are called to make it so. In other words—*compassion, comfort, healing,* and *restoration*—these actions, *too*, must always be with us. We must live with our hearts wide open:

> I will always guide you, I will walk with you.
> I will hold you in your deepest fear.
> I will give you life in all your empty places,
> with loving that treasures who you are:
> my prize, my beloved, my child.
>
> **("I WILL WALK WITH YOU," BY DAVID HAAS)**

The world says: How happy we are, and what a blessing it is to have our health, to be people who have our act together, where we can be worry-free. Jesus says: How happy and blessed they are, who have deep sorrow and are grieving, because true gladness is not far away from them.

What do we say? How will we choose to live?

BLEST

are they,

THE LOWLY ONES...

they

shall

INHERIT

the

earth.

> God is the one
> who is for me in this moment;
> every moment.
>
> **("EVERY MOMENT" BY DAVID HAAS)**

Many English

translations of the

Beatitudes translate this differently, and state it as, "blessed are the meek." It would be wrong for us to interpret this to mean that we are to be submissive, weak, passive, or silent. I would humbly suggest that Jesus has something completely different in mind, when speaking about the "lowly ones," the "*meek*." First, I would assert that what we are being called to, through this particular Beatitude, is to seek more of an *interior* life of self-reflection and discernment.

This is a call to be still, in prayer, and to *listen*. We often get it all wrong when it comes to prayer. We all have needs; we all bring them to prayer. We include these needs in our prayer, asking God to fix our problems, to solve our dilemmas, and to—if we are truly honest—do what *we* want God to do. I have often wondered that, again, if we were honest with ourselves, our preferred response to our Sunday communal prayers of petition would be, "We really, really want it—so give it to us now." We know what we want. We place it before God. We want God to respond according to *our* desires.

It is understandable that when we pray for a particular need that is not satisfied, we believe that God did not answer our prayer. But so often in our prayer *we* are doing all of the talking and we miss the fact that there is *always* an answer. God *always* responds. The first problem is we are not *listening*; and, secondly, we do not always like the answer! Pope Francis teaches us that there is a different path we can follow beyond those roads which have failed us in the past:

> Jesus proposes a different way of doing things: the way of meekness.
>
> Meekness is yet another expression of the interior poverty of those who put their trust in God alone... It is always better to be meek, for then our deepest desires will be fulfilled. The meek 'shall inherit the earth,' for they will see God's promises accomplished in their lives.
>
> Reacting with meekness and humility: that is holiness.
>
> **(GAUDETE ET EXSULTATE, 71, 74)**

The first two steps toward being "lowly" or "meek" in God's way, is to *listen more diligently* and to *accept with more surrender*. Prayer is most certainly speaking to God about what we want, and presenting to God our worries and concerns. But it is also—and in the end, much more important—our *listening* to what God is *trying to say to us*! Prayer is a conversation, *not* a monologue. We know that in our human relationships, a quality conversation cannot take place if only one is doing all the talking. We have to listen more diligently in prayer. Then, after clarifying God's voice, are we prepared to hear and accept God's "answer?" Prayer is speaking, then listening, and it requires a spirit of *surrender*. Surrender not only to what God might be leading us to do or choose, but also to surrender to the timeline and the nature of how this "answer" will be made known and realized. This is at the center of any kind of *discernment*, and most especially, in our discerning to discover what God wants of us.

Secondly, in the context of this understanding of "meekness" being an attitude and way of life that embraces *listening more diligently* and *accepting with more surrender*, is the acknowledgement and redirection of our understanding and commitment to how we live our faith—that to be lowly, one is never, ever, *passive*. To be meek is not to be submissive. There is absolutely no way we can follow Jesus and choose to be passive or submissive about anything around us, in our world, church, country, systems of government, families, and relationships, or within our relationship to and attitudes about ourselves. The lowly and the meek are *activists*. But this activism is not an arrogant kind of activism. This activism always acknowledges and surrenders to who God is and who we are not. It is to truly be humble, to submit ourselves to God's way, made known to us through Jesus. Jesus' way, while tender and "gentle of heart," is also courageous, strong yet always non-violent, always advocating for what is just, and continually preaching, teaching, and acting in God's name to help build the city of God, now—not later.

Beyond the witness of Jesus (which one could assert, should be enough), who are some role-models for us to embrace this particular understanding of meekness, or being a member of the "lowly ones?" Mahatma Gandhi, and the Rev. Dr. Martin Luther King, Jr., of course, come to mind. There are others: Archbishop Oscar Romero, Dorothy Day, Rutillio Grande, Cesar Chavez, Sr. Dorothy Stang, SNDdeN, Thomas Merton, Dan and Phillip Berrigan, Harvey Milk, Fr. Mychal Judge, and others who have gone before us. There are those who, today, are living the "meek" and "lowly" life in the Spirit of Jesus: Sr. Helen Prejean, Fr. Gregory Boyle, Shane Claiborne, Sr. Simone Campbell, Fr. John Dear, and so many more that we could name. These are all "saints" who refuse to give up on *love* as their instrument of conversion and change, who have lived to simply respond to God's way, to Jesus' way. This is not a separate activity from the life and practice of prayer that is being addressed here. Each and every day, might we consider taking some time to pull this "activism"—an activism of *love*—into our prayer, praise, rejoicing, and even our lament? It is so important. Like practicing a musical instrument, it requires patience and repetition. We have to be conscious in this blending of prayer and activism. It might seem difficult, but it is actually very simple. We need to "un-complicate" this by *moving and acting simply yet concretely.*

Let's not forget about the promise that such lowly ones will "inherit the earth." Do we want to inherit the earth as it presently stands? We don't like to face it, but we, as a planet, are on the edge of approaching global destruction in terms of how we are—or more accurately—are *not*—

caring for our planet. If we are going to take on the courageous and brave stance of being the meek—as Jesus would have us be—then we must without compromise, act accordingly as though we are not only stewards of the other wondrous creatures to whom God has given birth but also as the ecological stewards of and for one another. In the future, when we sing this verse of "Blest are They," let us call to mind all of creation and all its creatures. If we want to "inherit the earth," we must make commitments to *honor* the earth and the entire cosmos.

Rejoice and be glad! Why? Because we do not have to be famous like those named above, or amazing or otherworldly. What we need to do is to listen more diligently, accept and receive with more surrender, and move and act—simply yet concretely. Let's not try to do it all on our own. We need each other, and together we are called to serve as the family of Christ:

> Baptized in water,
> grafted to Jesus,
> sealed with the sign of grace,
> I am commissioned
> with all believers
> to show God's human face.
>
> **("BAPTIZED IN WATER," TEXT AND MUSIC BY JOHN BELL)**

This is one of the reasons that whenever I lead "Blest are They," whether it be at a liturgical celebration or at a concert, I have *everyone* gathered sing the lyrics "Blest are they the lowly ones, they shall inherit the earth." We do this *together*, although it will look different for each person.

Our unique personalities and human qualities will bring forward various ways of being meek, or of joining up with the lowly ones. We can most certainly inherit the earth when we are "grafted to Jesus," and then simply bring ourselves to the journey.

The world says: How happy we are, and what a blessing it is to be able to hold power, to be in charge and do whatever we want. Jesus says: How happy and blessed they are, who hold great humility because they will then inherit the joy of creation.

What do *we* say? How will *we* choose to live?

BLEST

are they who

HUNGER AND THIRST...

they shall

HAVE THEIR FILL.

There is
a temptation

when reading the Beatitudes to think of them as personal goals or spiritual exercises for the individual reflection of living life as viewed through the lens of faith. But, once again, as is the case with much of scripture, it is helpful to understand that the author of Matthew's Gospel is speaking to a *community*. While certainly the Beatitudes provide a path to examine our personal "right relationship with God," these proclamations are exactly that. Proclamations. *Public* proclamations. They are organizing principles for the Church, the Body of Christ.

I see now, all these years later, that this concluding phrase of the second verse of "Blest are They" misses the culmination of the exhortation. Looking back, I should have found a way to sing "Blest are they who hunger and thirst *for justice*." "Hindsight is 20/20," as the saying goes. I cannot change the text now, but what I can do, what we each can do, is to be intentional and mindful while singing this verse. Another way that many translations present this verse is, "... who hunger and thirst for *righteousness*."

Regardless, both of these key words, *justice* and *righteousness* and what they are announcing, are communal, even *universal* directives. They speak to us of our call to work toward the eradication of everything that is unjust:

social programs that harm the poor; economic policies that keep our sisters and brothers in poverty; all forms of discrimination based on one's color, gender, age, or sexual identity; politics that do not celebrate what Jim Wallis names as "*God's* politics." It is about getting to work and moving beyond being good or charitable, and to advocate for *true* systemic change so that all God's people can be the beneficiaries of God's holiness that is showered upon us all. It is to put some flesh on what we hear when each of us is named as "God's work of art" (Eph. 2:10).

When reflecting upon this responsibility, we can see that there is plenty of injustice to go around. Addressing this can lead to paralysis, where we end up doing nothing because the cause—or causes—for working toward justice seem(s) to be too many and too overwhelming. If we are going to be "Sermon on the Mount People," we have to find ways to melt away all that keeps us frozen. We have to ignite our passion so we can begin to shatter any form of injustice that is within our sight or reach: in the systems that determine how people live, in the structures of government that lock out and stigmatize those on the margins, and within the institutions—including church and other religious institutions—that, by their actions, or also by their complicity of silence, maintain an environment where a few are able to dominate and abuse their power over others. Pope Francis makes this very clear:

> Hunger and thirst are intense experiences, since they involve basic needs and our instinct for survival. There are those who desire justice and yearn for righteousness with similar intensity. Jesus says that

they will be satisfied, for sooner or later justice will come. We can cooperate to make that possible, even if we may not always see the fruit of our efforts.

True justice comes about in people's lives when they themselves are just in their decisions; it is expressed in their pursuit of justice for the poor and the weak. While it is true that the word "justice" can be a synonym for faithfulness to God's will in every aspect of our life, if we give the word too general a meaning, we forget that it is shown especially in justice towards those who are most vulnerable.

Hungering and thirsting for righteousness: that is holiness.

(GAUDETE ET EXSULTATE, 77, 79)

If we are attracted to and stirred by this call to holiness, then it is not optional to sit still. Christians are people who do not let up. We should strive to be a "broken record" for a world that does not want to hear our song of justice. Some may be OK with singing, smiling, and swaying while singing this verse of "Blest are They" (and this group would include me, at times), but we have to get beyond the words and notes that are in the hymnal. We have to sing this song *not* just during liturgy, but when and where people *need* to sing it, when they ache to be strengthened by it. While it certainly should be the case when singing all of the verses of "Blest are They," when we come to *this* verse, it should be a feast that fills and nourishes us to go forth from our tables to start feeding the world.

This is a matter of seeing our Lord not just as Jesus but as the *Christ*, the "anointed one." Jesus was anointed to bring hope and liberation. We are not off the hook here. Jesus' promise to the people who knew him is to be our promise to our sisters and brothers, right here and right now. As Teresa of Avila enlightens us: "There is no body now on earth but yours." We live in a time when more and more people claim to be "spiritual" but *not religious*. That is fine for a start. But after we gain some "spiritual self-actualization," then what? What will we do about it? Because this is a most *spiritual* matter, indeed! Being spiritual does not release us from a relationship with others. It is not a free pass to isolate ourselves from the cares and injustices of the world. Pierre Teilhard de Chardin once said, "We are not human *beings* having a *spiritual* experience; we are *spiritual beings* having a *human* experience."

The work to be done is not terribly mystical or laced with pious or spiritual thoughts. Justice is needed for the children who are dying of starvation. Justice is needed for those who are persecuted because of their sexual orientation. Justice is needed for the homeless and forgotten. Justice is needed for our elderly, who are the victims of policies which deprive them of their dignity. Justice is needed for a world who refuses to feed its people (especially when the resources are there to do so). Justice is needed for the suffering who cannot afford health care. Justice is needed for racial injustice. Justice is needed for the victims of human trafficking. Justice is needed for our planet that is facing catastrophic changes in the environment. Justice is needed for those immigrants and migrants seeking a better life and aching to belong to a more compassionate society. Justice is needed to cease the bombing, the raids, the missiles—and the guns—that are killing our people.

Rejoice and be glad! Why? Because Jesus has made a promise that it does not have to be this way. We have a most blessed opportunity to choose life by our standing up, by offering passionate resistance to the status quo. There can be a true meaning to our lives if we respond in compassion and with an energetic commitment. We can rejoice because in the end, truth wins out over lies. We can be glad because the *Bread of Life* nourishes and heals us from the food poisoning of injustice and hatred. We can rejoice and be glad because, as Archbishop Desmond Tutu has proclaimed:

> Goodness is stronger than evil;
> Love is stronger than hate;
> Light is stronger than darkness;
> Life is stronger than death.
> Victory is ours through him who loved us.
>
> **("GOODNESS IS STRONGER THAN EVIL," TEXT BY DESMOND TUTU, ADAPTED BY JOHN BELL; MUSIC BY JOHN BELL)**

The world says: How happy we are, and what a blessing it is to buy and consume whatever we choose, those who can enjoy all the comforts and pleasures of life. Jesus says: How happy and blessed they are who hunger, thirst, and ache for what is right because they will be fed and restored.

What do *we* say? How will *we* choose to live?

6

BLEST

are they who

SHOW MERCY...

mercy

SHALL BE THEIRS.

Not too long
after the official

conclusion of the Jubilee Year of Mercy that was proclaimed by Pope Francis, my good friend and ministry colleague Bill Huebsch was approached by a pastoral minister who asked, "OK, we spent this past year doing the 'mercy' thing. What's next?"

There is no "next." This is it. Mercy does not have a shelf-life stamped on it. It never expires. Beyond it arguably being the spiritual legacy of Pope Francis' pontificate, mercy is at the center of everything that has to do with Jesus—with being a Christian. To be merciful is to embrace the way of life steeped in Jesus. To be merciful is to take seriously that "nothing can separate us from the love of God" (Romans 8: 38). To be merciful is to practice this unconditional love with no strings attached, no exceptions and no distinctions. To follow this Beatitude means that we are committed to building a society of mercy, a world where forgiveness is immediate in its offer to another and boundless in its depth. To be merciful is to rid the world's lexicon of vengeful language and actions as well as from our hearts. As followers of Christ, we are especially called to forgive as a show of mercy, and to show this mercy to those whom we find it impossible or inconceivable to forgive.

Above any dogma or doctrine or catechism—teaching

the way of mercy should be the beginning, middle, and end of the curriculum we teach our children. It is also at the center of our mission and message. The announcement of the mercy of God is more important than any programmatic "new evangelization," as *mercy* is to be the proclamation that can never be shouted loud enough or sung more passionately. We do not go to school to learn this important charism. We have to begin with ourselves, and participate in an examination of our lives. It comes down to this: We all want and desire mercy and forgiveness. Jesus makes this clear in announcing his mission to "desire mercy, not sacrifice" (Matt. 9:13). We must start from within by first accepting God's astonishing forgiveness toward us; then in that spirit we begin the journey of forgiving *ourselves*. Only then can we understand the unselfish nature of giving freely while expecting nothing in return. Only after taking part in this daily practice, can we begin to forgive others as we are directed to do so in the Sermon on the Mount. Jesus had in his backpack of wisdom the gentle dogma so powerfully articulated in Psalm 103, paraphrased here:

> You God,
> You God, who forgives everything,
> who heals everything,
> who redeems everything,
> who crowns everything with a tireless love;
> who satisfies;
> who is kind and full of mercy,
> who awakens and refreshes all time
> and continually buds forth the feather of an eagle—

forever young.
You are forever full of promise.

You God,
You God, who is just when everything
and everyone else seems unjust.

You: kindness.
Graciousness. Mercy.
Anger falls away.
Love enters, new and bright.
You dwell with us, not accusing;
refusing to haunt us with our sin.
Never returning our brokenness with more brokenness.

As high as the heaven can possibly be above this earth,
so far and wide is your kindness.

You God,
you God, who transforms our weakness
from one far end to the other,
are always healing, always loving,
Our failings are sent so very far away.

As a parent, ever so compassionate,
you God,
you God, re-define and re-create compassion.

You God,
You God, you know who we are;
never forgetting we are like the dust,
and the dry grass,
pushing out the flower in the field,
for only wind passes through,

and it is gone.
The field—quickly forgets.

But you God,
your love stretches and looms
from forever to forever.
From you, righteousness flows from us
to our children,
and our children's children—
for those who keep faith with you;
for those who keep moving with you.

You, God.
You God, sit high while looking low,
deep into the center of all things,
embracing everything,
blessing everything and everyone.

(FROM PSALM 103, PARA. FROM "MY HEART IS READY: PSALM-POEMS FOR PRAYER AND PROCLAMATION" BY DAVID HAAS)

We need to surrender to the truth that comes from God—that no one is unworthy to receive this gift. No one is to be denied. There is nothing too awful, too horrific, too heinous, or too disgusting that will keep us from the merciful love of God. Why is this concept so hard? I believe that the root of our inability to forgive is a deep *fear* that leads to the hardening of our hearts. We are afraid to forgive others and to forgive ourselves. It might be rooted in the fear that if we are vulnerable and courageous enough to offer such forgiveness and mercy, then we can no longer remain entrenched in the quicksand. It means, then, that we have to break free, get up, and truly live. We have to release our anger and move toward healing in our lives. It means that we reject lives of shame and punishment. It means that we exorcise our resentments and the need for revenge. Instead, *love* will be the response that we offer in all things. We are being invited daily to surrender and celebrate what I have come to call the *God of Second Chances*:

> Come now, O God of Second Chances;
> open our lives to heal.
> Remove our hate and melt our rage.
> Save us from ourselves.
>
> Come now, O God, release our demons;
> open our eyes to see
> the shame within, our guilt and pain.
> Mend us, make us whole.
>
> Come now, O God, and still our anger;
> open our minds to peace.
> Embrace our fear and hold us close.
> Calm the storm within.
>
> Come now, O God, shake our resentment;
> open our way to choose
> the way of love over revenge.
> Show us a new way.
>
> Come now, O God, and grant compassion;
> open our hearts to love.
> May we let go of all our hurt.
> Help us to move on.
>
> Come now, O God of Second Chances;

may we forgive ourselves.
May we become your living sign:
Children of God's love.

**("THE GOD OF SECOND CHANCES,"
TEXT AND MUSIC BY DAVID HAAS)**

Still, to this day, whenever I come to the beginning of the third verse of "Blest are They" (*Blest are they, who show mercy...*), I feel a bit sad. When I was a child, I remember my parents and others who tried to console me when I was bullied by encouraging me to embrace the old saying, "Sticks and stones may break my bones, but words will never hurt me." While well intentioned, it never helped. The words *did* matter; the bruises remained. Some of them still do. More bruises continue to come and cut into my spiritual skin, as I am sure they do in some fashion, for each of us. In some ways I have found healing in both the memories and current struggles, yet in other instances the pain still lingers.

I don't know why, exactly. Maybe it is because I really have not fully accepted the mercy freely given that is named in the *God of Second Chances* in my own life, and I certainly know that I do not offer the same mercy, the same second chance to those in my life for whom I still hold hard feelings. Like many of us, I still have feelings of needing to make restitution in some way, and that any forgiveness I need or seek to give others needs to be *earned*. Pope Francis addresses this:

Mercy has two aspects. It involves giving, helping and serving others, but it also includes forgiveness and understanding.

Giving and forgiving means reproducing in our lives some small measure of God's perfection, which gives and forgives superabundantly.... The yardstick we use for understanding and forgiving others will measure the forgiveness we receive. The yardstick we use for giving will measure what we receive. We should never forget this.

Jesus does not say, "Blessed are those who plot revenge." He calls "blessed" those who forgive and do so, "seventy times seven" (Matt. 18:22). We need to think of ourselves as an army of the forgiven. All of us have been looked upon with divine compassion.

Seeing and acting with mercy: that is holiness.

(GAUDETE ET EXSULTATE, 80-82)

Pope Francis is teaching us that mercy is the way of God. This mercy holds power—a power of compassion that can cut through everything. As our own wounds and those we wish upon others go deep, we are being called to a prayer for God to fill us with an overabundance of love and compassion, and to not let up in opening our hearts to accept and to become this very love ourselves. As the hymn already cited acknowledges, there is a "storm within" that only God can calm. We each have some degree of the darkness within us, tempting us to judge, condemn, strike out or strike back, or to cause harm for some vile motivation to soothe ourselves. This is at the very heart of our inability to show mercy and offer forgiveness. It is often because we cannot forgive ourselves, we cannot soften the harshness that rises in our hearts, and so, out of personal frustration and shame, we need to dump it on others.

Like all the other Beatitudes, this one requires a lot of work. It does not, and will not, come quickly. Once again, it must be practiced diligently. A path forward and through for each of us might be to intentionally seek out practicing the *works* of mercy (see Mt. 25:31-36 to examine the biblical roots of the works of mercy). May we each find some ways that we can be concretely involved in actions of feeding the hungry, visiting the poor and imprisoned, and finding ways to bring clothing and warmth to the naked; to be actively "pro-life" in all of the realities that work against life: working for an end to abortion *and* the death penalty, and pushing relentlessly for an end to policies that encourage and perpetuate gun violence; speaking out on behalf of the marginalized; finding a home and "being" home for the homeless; visiting the sick, or to "take all the lost home:"

> Take all the lost home,
> remember their names all,
> their journey is yours, friend.
> Their faces are grey 'till you call.
>
> Walk close by the children
> and learn their refrains,
> and leave your umbrellas
> while you learn to walk in the rain.
>
> Remember the one cup you share in my name.
> The wine and the water are one and the same,
> all the same.

Comfort the old ones,
be tender and strong;
rekindle their tired dreams
and sing them your song, sing your song.

The bread that is broken won't be one again,
unless in your healing you gather each one and
each grain.

Take all the lost home,
walk close by the children,
and comfort the old ones
'till I come again, come again.

**("TAKE ALL THE LOST HOME,"
TEXT AND MUSIC BY JOE WISE)**

Rejoice and be glad! Why? Because this gift of mercy is not as far away as we might think. It is hidden—but not absent. We can find joy because, while it can seem so hard to practice, the process and attitude of mercy is a way for us to grow closer to God. It is the very breath that comes from God's lungs and heart. The world says: How happy we are, and what a blessing it is to always be right and to sit in judgment over others and determine their outcome. Jesus says: How happy and blessed they are who are filled with mercy, whose lives overflow with lavish forgiveness, for they too will receive the same mercy.

What do *we* say? How will *we* choose to live?

7

BLEST

are they,

THE PURE OF

HEART...

they shall

SEE GOD.

This particular

Beatitude may be

among the most difficult. It seems so impossible. We all strive to be good, to be better people. We want our motives, choices, and intentions to be "pure," but they can become tainted so easily. It seems to be second nature for infants and small children, but around age four or five it begins to slowly wither away. It would be easy to believe that Abraham Lincoln's famous admonition of "malice toward none and charity for all" might not be very welcomed in today's society. Yet, hardened hearts and darkened souls are a result of learned behavior, but, with the grace of God, can be unlearned. This is the struggle and invitation to be pure and harvest a "clean heart," so knowingly prayed for in Psalm 51:

> Make clean and clear away
> all of the dust and debris from my heart.
> Come and bring a steadiness,
> a smooth path to my spirit.
>
> Do not abandon me –
> keep me tight to your presence.
>
> Help me,
> convince me that joy will follow pain.

Sustain and support me;
and know that I will provide the direction
for those who need to return to you.

Stop the tears
so I will be able to sing a song
love-packed with the taste of you.
Provide for my voice
to clearly become a shout of praise to you.

Courage.
Bring courage to my heart.

Sacrifices will not work.
They do not satisfy you.
So then,
I offer you my broken self;
my fragile heart, my tender spirit.

These things you welcome.

You will not turn away,
because you have my heart.

(FROM PSALM 51: 12-19, PARA. FROM "MY HEART IS READY: PSALM-POEMS FOR PRAYER AND PROCLAMATION" BY DAVID HAAS)

To achieve purity of heart requires a certain level of what is so typically called "inner peace." We desperately long for contentment, but for it to arrive in our hearts it seems to require that we almost live our lives in a plastic bubble so that nothing will enter our hearts to contaminate it. We read that love is "patient," "kind," "never boastful," and so on (see 1 Cor. 13: 1-13). Well, who do we know "out there" besides Jesus himself who has ever accomplished such a goal? So many times when we try to act based on pure motives with this "clean heart," things can go awry and actually get worse. It becomes very easy for us to cast judgment on others (whom we deem less worthy than ourselves), knowing full well how far away we are from embracing such contentment and pure love ourselves.

The word and image of purity is problematic because it is so often associated with the notion of being perfect. We need to soften expectations we have for ourselves— and others—in this journey toward purity of heart because to take this notion literally will immediately invite failure. The move toward clean hearts, from the point of view of the Sermon on the Mount, is about reaching out to *expand* our hearts, widening them to be more accessible and open to share with others. Working toward achieving a clean and pure heart needs to be seen as a journey; we will never reach its final destination on this earth, but while on the road we do get a little closer. The covenant that comes to us again and again from the Hebrew scriptures can help clarify—when the announcement is made several times, "I will be your God, and you will be my people" (Jer. 7:23). God never says, "I will be your God, and you will be my series of individual and interpersonal relationships." God has a heart that is *huge*—large enough to take us all in, and this God hugs and embraces each of us in this expansive chamber of love. To have a pure heart is to revel in a loving relationship, a love of God, and an ever increasing love of our sisters and brothers, as Pope Francis teaches:

A heart capable of love admits nothing that might harm, weaken or endanger that love. The Bible uses the heart to describe our real intentions, the things we truly seek and desire, apart from all appearances... God wants to speak to our hearts...

The Lord expects a commitment to our brothers and sisters that comes from the heart...

A heart that loves God and neighbor (cf. Mt. 22:36-40), genuinely and not merely in words, is a pure heart; it can see God...to the extent that truth and love prevail, we will then be able to see "face to face." Jesus promises that those who are pure in heart "will see God."

Keeping a heart free of all that tarnishes love: that is holiness.

(GAUDETE ET EXSULTATE, 83, 85-86)

There it is! Pope Francis has named it. This is what it means to be "pure of heart," to keep our hearts clean and "free of all that tarnishes love." This is the revolutionary announcement of Jesus—he is not interested in our achieving perfection. What he *is* interested in, and very passionately so, is our commitment to the covenant, which is to acknowledge that any kind of love that has value *comes from God*. Our calling or vocation is to discern and choose *how* we will respond to this love. Too much religion—including Christianity—seems to focus on obedience, following the teaching and the "rules" of making sure every minute liturgical rubric is followed, and of never straying from the "pure" *moral* life. Not so with Jesus, and it should be the same for us. It is entirely and completely about the cause of love. God's love. A love that is everlasting. A love that keeps our hearts in shape. A heart filled with a love that refuses to value anything that speaks of hate, violence, revenge, or any other kind of harm. To claim to be a Christian means that there can be no room for anything which promotes such things.

To embrace the "pure" and "clean" heart means that we not only accept but celebrate the glorious gift that everyone is capable and worthy of love; we are each the "beloved." *Every single one of us* is a precious and wonderful child of God. If we can predicate every action and choice with this fundamental stance, then the failures, vulnerabilities, flaws, shortcomings, and, yes—even the annoying personality traits—fall away. What we then choose to see is a temple of beauty and goodness. You and I. Each other. All of us.

Rejoice and be glad! Why? Because when we can expand our hearts to see *each other* as beloved children of God, then we can, as the Beatitude concludes, actually "see God." This is why at the end of the verse when the words proclaim "they shall see God," there is an exclamation point at the end with the sung words being *accented*. That was on purpose because I hope the verse can help us to rejoice! When we can have hearts opened to receive this truth, then we do not limit the presence of Jesus to the tabernacle, or the spoken and preached word, or in other sacramental signs and wonders—as fantastic as they all are. We will then be able to *see*, without reserve, or condition or modification, the presence of God in each other, in *human beings*, as John Foley so beautifully paraphrased years ago:

We hold a treasure not made of gold;
in earthen vessels wealth untold.
One treasure only, the Lord, the Christ,
in earthen vessels.

("EARTHEN VESSELS," TEXT AND MUSIC BY JOHN FOLEY, SJ)

Yes, we are sinners. But we need to relentlessly remind ourselves that God loves sinners! May God bless the life and memory of Henri Nouwen, who never tired of reminding us that we are the beloved daughters and sons of God. We are each "somebody" in the eyes of God!

I am, I am the beloved of God.
All of us, all are beloved of God,
not for what we do,
but because of who God says we are.
We are the beloved of God.

("THE BELOVED OF GOD," INSPIRED BY HENRI J. M. NOUWEN; WORDS AND MUSIC BY DAVID HAAS)

The world says: How happy we are, and what a blessing it is to be able to utilize any approach at our finger tips to decimate and shame our enemies and those who do not ascribe to our way of looking at the world—to always be able to win. Jesus says: How happy and blessed they are, who begin each day striving to have clean hearts and choose goodness over achieving false victory.

What do *we* say? How will *we* choose to live?

BLEST

are they who

SEEK PEACE...

they are the

CHILDREN OF GOD.

Tremble, but do not be afraid.
Be attentive to your heart,
and be peaceful throughout the night.

("BE PEACEFUL" BY DAVID HAAS)

There is no

fancy, elaborate,

or lofty way to say it otherwise: We are called by Jesus to
be *peacemakers*. When he appears to the apostles in the
upper room, in the midst of their fear, his first word to them
is "peace" (John 20: 26). So why do we seem to habitually
fail to practice this commandment, this central teaching of
the Risen Lord?

We really are inclined to walk away from being peacemakers. It can be very easy to manipulate and misspeak
the message of Jesus when he says, "I am the peace the
world cannot give" (John 14:27) because we take this too
literally. True, the world as we know it cannot bring about
the genuine peace of God, especially when our efforts are
brought about by force, often through war. But here is what
we *need* to claim: when we "put on Christ" we *are* no longer
of this world. When we "put on Christ" and follow the path
of peace, then we are the *very presence* of Christ. We can
and must "put on" being *peacemakers* as well.

So then, how do we embrace this call to be peacemakers? It is really quite simple (but it is also very hard). The bottom line is that we do not kill anyone. No exceptions. Period. Stop the killing. There is no reason to take another life. Do we sometimes feel the need for revenge when someone kills and takes a human life? Do we justify an "eye for an eye" when a horrible injustice has befallen someone we love? Such feelings are certainly understandable. But no matter how angry, hurt, grief-stricken or rage-filled we are, we simply do not reciprocate. *We don't kill.*

It also means that war is *never* an option. In the vision of Jesus, war is unacceptable, intolerable, and in no way an action of God. If we are Christians, according to Jesus, we simply do not take part in war. We do not support it, we do not approve of law makers who budget money for war, and we do not participate in it. Our God is one of peace. Jesus is the *Prince of Peace*. How could he be the *Prince of Peace* if he were to promote war?

In addition, it means that we do not approve of citizens owning or using guns manufactured for the single purpose of killing. Jesus couldn't care less about the Second Amendment or any manipulated interpretation of it. Jesus couldn't care less about anyone's desire to have "fun" by going to the range to "shoot." Jesus not only doesn't promote the owning and use of weapons but he simply does not tolerate it. He commands Peter to put away the sword (John 18:10-11). This may make some people angry because they believe they should be able to have "fun" with their guns. Having fun is a great thing. We should all have fun! But why with a gun? Do something else. Bowling is fun! Water skiing is fun! Going to the movies is fun! How about having this type of fun with family and friends? The way of Jesus?—No guns. No weapons.

To be the Church, the "Body of Christ," means that we can no longer support any kind of violence or killing. It simply is not of God. Read the Beatitude again—or rather, the next time you sing this verse of "Blest are They" pay attention: "Blest are they who seek peace, they are the children of God." How else are we to read this? Do we think, "Well, Jesus isn't talking about *me* and *my* gun..." (actually, he is). Or do we think, "Well, it's a nice thought, but naïve and unrealistic." Jesus really *does* mean this. No killing. No weapons. No more promotion or taking part in war. No more violence. Enough!

It does not end here. In being called to be peacemakers, we need to disengage ourselves from any kind of violence: physical, emotional, psychological, or spiritual. Physical or sexual abuse, torture, bullying, psychological or emotional abuse, goading, verbal abuse, gossip, ridicule or extreme teasing—we are to use every spiritual power we can access—through the power of the Spirit of God—not to take part in, engage in, or promote such behavior. It is a call to be transformed and to become instruments of peace:

> Make me an instrument of your peace, O God.
> Make me an instrument of your peace.
>
> Where there is hatred, let me be love.
> Where there is injury, let me show pardon.
> Where there is doubt, let me sing faith to all.
> Make me your instrument.
>
> Where there's despair, let me bring hope.

Where there is darkness let me be your light.
Where there is sadness, let me be radiant with joy.
Make me your instrument.

Grant, O God, that I may never seek
so much to be consoled as to console;
not to be understood as to understand;
not to be loved, but to love.

It is in giving that we receive.
It is in forgiving where we are forgiven.
It is in dying that we are born to eternal life.
Make me your instrument.

("AN INSTRUMENT OF YOUR PEACE" TEXT ATTRIBUTED TO ST. FRANCIS OF ASSISI; MUSIC AND TEXT ADAPTATION BY DAVID HAAS)

Pope Francis would agree:

This Beatitude makes us think of the many endless situations of war in our world. Yet we ourselves are often a cause of conflict.... The world of gossip, inhabited by negative and destructive people, does not bring peace. Such people are really the enemies of peace; in no way are they "blessed."

Peacemakers truly "make" peace; they build peace and friendship in society. To those who sow peace Jesus makes this magnificent promise: "They will be called children of God" (Mt. 5:9).

It is not easy to "make" this evangelical peace, which excludes no one but embraces even those who are a bit odd, troublesome or difficult, demanding, different, beaten down by life or simply uninterested. It is hard work; it calls for a great openness of mind and heart.... We need to be artisans of peace, for building peace is a craft that demands serenity, creativity, sensitivity and skill.

Sowing peace all around us: that is holiness.

(GAUDETE ET EXSULTATE, 87-89)

This is not easy. I violate these principles all the time, and every time I do, I need to repent, seek forgiveness from God and others, and go back to square one. I am a Christian. Jesus asks a lot from Christians. It is difficult, and I need sisters and brothers to practice this Christianity with me. I often do not like what I sometimes consider to be constraints. I want to lash out, and I am sad to admit that I do seek revenge at times. There are times when I am a terrible gossip. While I have never owned a weapon or taken part in any overt violent acts, when I search my heart, I know there are times when I have wished for harm upon someone else. When I have been hurt by people, I want them to be hurt in return. But I have a problem here. I am a Christian. I am called and even commanded to choose differently, to act differently, to *live* differently. When I sing the verse "Blest are they who seek peace," I am committing myself again to try, to really try, and get whatever help I can to soften hateful, angry, even violent thoughts that often fill my mind. If I am a child of God, then I need to do everything I can to live as one with everyone around me. That means I seek peace with everything

I think, say, do, and with everything I bring to my leadership in sung prayer.

Rejoice and be glad! Why? Despite how unbelievably difficult it is to make such radical transformations in our beliefs, attitudes, and actions, it is wonderful that we have a God who is so unconditionally "pro-life" in everything! It is refreshing that this God of ours is consistent and unyielding in the way we are to live. God certainly forgives us when we fall short, as we all should. But God continually wants us to get up, start over, try again, and never seems to give up on us. God really believes in the possibilities that we can develop to become peacemakers. God has faith in us that we want to change the rising tide of violence in the world. From this moment forward—knowing full well that we will stumble and fall short—let's keep the goal ever before us to be instruments of peace:

> Peace before us, peace behind us,
> peace under our feet.
> Peace within us, peace over us,
> let all around us be peace.
>
> **("PRAYER FOR PEACE," BY DAVID HAAS)**

The world says: How happy we are, and what a blessing it is to always beat others down, or to always win. Jesus says: How happy and blessed they are, who are always seeking peace, for they belong to God as the beloved daughters and sons of God.

What do *we* say? How will *we* choose to live?

BLEST

are they who

SUFFER IN FAITH,

the glory of God

IS THEIRS...

Blest are you

WHO SUFFER HATE,

all because of me.

> Neither death nor life,
> the past nor things to come;
> will ever bring your harm
> or keep you from God's love.

(FROM "NEITHER DEATH NOR LIFE" BY DAVID HAAS)

To follow Jesus authentically, we

need to become risk-takers. These risks require us to invest our faith in a God who might seem, when reflecting on these concluding blessings, as a bit masochistic. Why would we want to suffer? Why would we choose to be persecuted? Is there another option besides being martyred? How can any kind of suffering be seen as something blessed?

How quickly we forget. Each of the Beatitudes that has led us to this point is steeped deeply in suffering and persecution for both Jesus and his followers. Each of the attributes being praised in these pages begins with a risk, and concludes, that if we take any of them seriously, it comes with a price. There are consequences for being a "Sermon on the Mount People." Submitting ourselves over to God's way, vision, and path means that we are saying "No" to values and principles that are all too common, and very much valued and rewarded by our culture.

We also might find it either ironic or contradictory that the Beatitude immediately preceding this one promotes peacemaking. If we step into this Beatitude of suffering after reveling in the vision of peace, it might seem to be a very abrupt turnaround, one that may tempt us to go running back to where and how we lived before. If we promote the values of the Beatitudes, the first response from most people will not be, "Thank you for sharing." Quite to the contrary, we will most likely be made fun of, criticized, called naïve, or childish, utopian, or at worst, stupid and crazy. In our country, many people may harass our way of thinking. In other countries and cultures, people can literally be murdered for holding such beliefs. People have been assassinated here in the United States for promoting such beliefs, like Dr. Martin Luther King, Jr., Bobby Kennedy, and other less public figures. But now we are being invited to embrace these pearls of wisdom and take up the mantle of mission. I have always been struck that, whenever I sing and lead "Blest are They," the final verse moves from "Blest are they..." to "Blest are *you*." That would mean you and me.

Most societies and cultures—as well as the Church, upon occasions—do not hold up the teachings of the Beatitudes. We live in a time when more than ever success, power, wealth, and achieving celebrity status are valued much more than being "poor in spirit," "meek," people who "hunger and thirst for justice," or "forgive unconditionally" or who want to be "peace-seekers." So, we most certainly will be persecuted, ridiculed, or disregarded by many for our attempts to follow the Jesus who teaches the Sermon on the Mount.

Jesus' entire life was woven with suffering. Daily he

was mocked, suspected, hated, and eventually betrayed; he was denied and shamed, leading ultimately to his execution. The entire public ministry of Jesus warns us that we will meet opposition, oppression, and ridicule. We are warned over and over again that to follow him will lead to our own suffering and potential martyrdom. Pope Francis makes this clear, as well:

> Jesus himself warns us that the path he proposes goes against the flow, even making us challenge society by the way we live and, as a result, becoming a nuisance. He reminds us how many people have been, and still are, persecuted simply because they struggle for justice, because they take seriously their commitment to God and to others. Unless we want to sink in an obscure mediocrity, let us not long for an easy life, for "whoever would save his life will lose it" (Mt. 16:25).

> Whatever weariness and pain we may experience in living the commandment of love and following the way of justice, the cross remains the source of our growth and sanctification.... Here we are speaking about inevitable persecution, not the kind of persecution we might bring upon ourselves by the mistreatment of others.

> Persecutions are not a reality of the past, for today too we experience them, whether by the shedding of blood, as is the case with so many contemporary martyrs, or by subtle means, by slander and lies. Jesus calls us blessed when people "utter all kinds of evil against you falsely on my account" (Mt. 5:11).

Accepting daily the path of the Gospel, even though it may cause us problems: that is holiness.

(GAUDETE ET EXSULTATE, 90, 92-94)

The composers of the recent hit movie musical, "The Greatest Showman," would agree with this most passionate proclamation of how God wants the suffering and the marginalized to see and celebrate who they are:

I am not a stranger to the dark
Hide away, they say
'Cause we don't want your broken parts.
I've learned to be ashamed of all my scars.
Run away, they say,
no one'll love you as you are.

But I won't let them break me down to dust.
I know that there's a place for us.
For we are glorious.

When the sharpest words wanna cut me down,
I'm gonna send a flood, gonna drown them out.
I am brave, I am bruised
I am who I'm meant to be, this is me.

Look out 'cause here I come,
and I'm marching on to the beat I drum
I'm not scared to be seen -
I make no apologies, this is me.

Another round of bullets hits my skin.
Well, fire away 'cause today, I won't let the shame sink in.

We are bursting through the barricades
and reaching for the sun—we are warriors—
yeah, that's what we've become.

I won't let them break me down to dust.
I know that there's a place for us.
For we are glorious.
When the sharpest words wanna cut me down,
I'm gonna send a flood, gonna drown them out.
I am brave, I am bruised.
I am who I'm meant to be, this is me.

Look out 'cause here I come
And I'm marching on to the beat I drum
I'm not scared to be seen
I make no apologies, this is me.

This is me,
and I know that I deserve your love
'cause there's nothing I'm not worthy of.

When the sharpest words wanna cut me down,
I'm gonna send a flood, gonna drown them out.
This is brave, this is proof -
This is who I'm meant to be, this is me.

Look out 'cause here I come -
And I'm marching on to the beat I drum.
I'm not scared to be seen
I make no apologies, this is me.

**("THIS IS ME" FROM *THE GREATEST SHOWMAN*. MUSIC
AND LYRICS BY JUSTIN PAUL AND BENJ PASEK)**

(Songwriters: Justin Paul / Benj Pasek "This Is Me" lyrics © Sony/ATV
Music Publishing, LLC; Kobalt Music Publishing, Ltd.)

Rejoice and be glad! Why? Because while we travel this road of suffering and persecution, we can hold on to the truth that we are in good company. We are not alone. Jesus walks with us. The program that he lays out in the Beatitudes, while painful, is also filled with joy and glory, with love being the banner that we wave. The Beatitudes are a high calling and filled with blessed wisdom, so with courage we can endure and rise again. We are called to give of ourselves, our very lives—for what the School Sisters of Notre Dame sing and pray, almost on a daily basis:

> God's cause is the only concern of our hearts.
> God's cause is our cause.
>
> **("GOD'S CAUSE," TEXT BY BLESSED THERESA GER-HARDINGER, ADAPTATION AND MUSIC BY DAVID HAAS)**

The world says: How happy we are, and what a blessing it is to have no constraints on our lives whatsoever, and who are totally free. Jesus says: How happy and blessed they are, who suffer from oppression and are bullied—all because they seek justice, for they will always dwell in God's house. The world also says: How happy we are, and what a blessing it is to be admired and popular among the masses, who enjoy the benefits of having a wonderful reputation and universal esteem. But Jesus says: How happy and blessed they are who are continually insulted, mocked, or gossiped about and falsely accused because they choose God's way, for they will ultimately rejoice and be glad, for the ultimate prize awaits them—being one with God.

What do *we* say? How will *we* choose to live?

REJOICE

AND

BE GLAD!

1

Years ago,

Kurt Vonnegut

provided his perspective:

> "For some reason, the most vocal Christians among us never mention the Beatitudes (Matthew 5). But, often with tears in their eyes, they demand that the Ten Commandments be posted in public buildings. And of course, that's Moses, not Jesus. I haven't heard one of them demand that the Sermon on the Mount, the Beatitudes, be posted anywhere. 'Blessed are the merciful' in a courtroom? 'Blessed are the peacemakers' in the Pentagon? Give me a break!"

The question that I have been trying to address throughout these pages, and that I find myself asking is this: Why should we "rejoice and be glad?" What is the rejoicing and gladness which this refrain keeps erupting with after each verse? Where can it be found? How am I—or even more importantly, how are we—"blessed and holy?" Is this really the case?

While it is always a bit presumptuous to prophecy what Jesus might say today on whatever "mount" we might gather around, Nadia Bolz-Weber gives us a suggestion about how he might have preached to us—or perhaps, *is preaching to us now* through his present-day ambassadors— in our present circumstances:

> "Blessed are the poor in spirit, for theirs is the kingdom of heaven. Blessed are the agnostics. Blessed are they who doubt. Those who aren't sure, who can still be surprised. Blessed are they who are spiritually impoverished and therefore not so certain about everything that they no longer take in as new information. Blessed are those who have nothing to offer. Blessed are they for whom nothing seems to be working. Blessed are the pre-schoolers who cut in line at communion. Blessed are the poor in spirit. You are of heaven and Jesus blesses you.

> "Blessed are those who mourn, for they will be comforted. Blessed are they for whom death is not an abstraction. Blessed are they who have buried their loved ones, for whom tears are as real as an ocean. Blessed are they who have loved enough to know what loss feels like. Blessed are the mothers of the miscarried. Blessed are they who don't have the luxury of taking things for granted. Blessed are they who can't fall apart because they have to keep it together for everyone else. Blessed are the motherless, the alone, the ones from whom so much has been taken. Blessed are those who "still aren't over it yet." Blessed are they who laughed again when for so long they thought they never would. Blessed are Bo's wife and kids and Billy's mom and Amy Mac's

friends. Blessed are those who mourn. You are of heaven and Jesus blesses you.

"Blessed are the meek, for they will inherit the earth. Blessed are those who no one else notices. The kids who sit alone at middle-school lunch tables. The laundry guys at the hospital. The sex-workers and the night shift street sweepers. Blessed are the losers and the babies and the parts of ourselves that are so small. The parts of ourselves that don't want to make eye contact with a world that only loves the winners. Blessed are the forgotten. Blessed are the closeted. Blessed are the unemployed, the unimpressive, the underrepresented. Blessed are the teens who have to figure out ways to hide the new cuts on their arms. Blessed are the meek. You are of heaven and Jesus blesses you.

"Blessed are those who hunger and thirst for righteousness, for they will be filled. Blessed are the wrongly accused, the ones who never catch a break, the ones for whom life is hard—for they are those with whom Jesus chose to surround himself. Blessed are those without documentation. Blessed are the ones without lobbyists. Blessed are foster kids and trophy kids and special-ed kids and every other kid who just wants to feel safe and loved but never does. Blessed are those who hunger and thirst for righteousness. Blessed are they who know there has to be more than this. Because they are right.

"Blessed are the merciful, for they will receive mercy.

Blessed are those who make terrible business decisions for the sake of people. Blessed are the burnt-out social workers and the over-worked teachers and the pro-bono case takers. Blessed are the kids who step between the bullies and the weak. Blessed are they who delete hateful, homophobic comments off their friend's Facebook page. Blessed are the ones who have received such real grace that they are no longer in the position of ever deciding who the "deserving poor" are. Blessed is everyone who has ever forgiven me when I didn't deserve it. Blessed are the merciful for they totally get it."

Yes, it really is true. God is so delighted with us, so much in love with us—that God cannot be for us anything but this vital promise for a world taken up with the vision of the Beatitudes. This is what the "blessedness" of the Beatitudes lays out for us. This is true holiness—not the perfected achievement of accomplishing all that the Sermon on the Mount asks of us. Holiness is found when we make the journey, when we follow on the path. Maybe this is why the Holy Spirit led the reformers of the Lectionary years ago to appoint Matthew's Beatitudes as the Gospel reading for the Feast of All Saints. Saints are not those who achieve sacred perfection—saints are sinful, broken, hurting, flawed, and vulnerable people who want to make the journey and embrace the adventure. Arriving at the destination without struggle is not what is being asked of us. Let us leave that to God.

Years ago, a student of mine said to me: "I don't like going to church because they are all hypocrites." I responded that yes, this is often true. But we need to think on this—saying that everyone who goes to church should not be hypocritical is the same as saying that everyone who goes to "Weight Watchers" should be thin! The reason why we rejoice and are glad is that we are not alone. None of us are truly "thin"— we are all "overweight" and falling short. But we hold on to this promise: We will not be left for dead. Hope is to be found in God's way. Yes—God's way.

Wanda Landowska (1879-1959) was a Polish-French harpsichordist who ushered in a renewed popularity of the harpsichord in the 20th century and was a highly regarded authority on the music and interpretation of Johann Sebastian Bach. She once said, "You play Bach your way, and I will play Bach *his* way." Jesus is proclaiming a similarly parallel message to all who desire to follow: "You follow God *your* way—with your moral and pious relativism—but I am going to follow God in *God's* way."

While I do not claim to be Bach, I hope and pray that whenever we sing "Blest are They" we will find a path to rediscover, or perhaps for some of us, come to know for the first time, *God's way*. Through God's way, the "poor in spirit" find their home again after it has been obliterated through storms and hurricanes. Those "full of sorrow" will know comfort after burying a loved one. The "lowly ones" will find their voice once again and be heard. Those "who hunger and thirst" will find clarity in their paths of discernment and be led to a life of justice and righteousness. Those "who show mercy" will be front and center of God's proclamation that mercy is not reduced to a Jubilee year, but rather, a way of life to follow relentlessly. The "pure of heart" will be affirmed in their teaching the rest of us how to hold the hands and hearts of those on the walk who are broken, so that all of us can celebrate a God who promises to never leave us alone—and "see God." Those "who seek peace" will see some of their dreams come true, by continually revealing to us an alternative way of speaking and living that will one day see hearts melted beyond the addiction to our own way of thinking. Those "who suffer in faith" will be rewarded not for having to *defend the faith* but for saying yes to the basic vocation of following Jesus, which, in the words of Henri Nouwen, means becoming "a living witness of God's love." The ones who "suffer hate" because of their commitment to following Jesus will know that they were not misguided for doing so, and that everything Jesus taught, preached, proclaimed, died, and rose for is real. Because of this, these saints of God—and each of us—will be able to "rejoice and be glad." We cannot come close to doing so authentically unless we enter into, as I suggested in the introduction of this book, both an individual and collective examination of conscience.

A few years ago after a parish concert I presented, a woman came up to me and said, "I just love 'Blest are They.' What a great song! How did you come up with those words?" I chuckled and replied to her gently that it was Jesus of Nazareth presented by Matthew the Evangelist who "wrote the words," *not* David of Bridgeport, Michigan, the fledgling liturgical composer attempting to break open and celebrate these words. Even though I "wrote the song," I did not compose the message, nor did I ignite the mission. I need to recommit myself—every time I sing and lead this song—to the announcement presented in these words that

I had the audacity to set to music. I need to *decrease* any pride that may fill my heart and mind as being the "composer" and *increase* Jesus.

We are each being charged with taking on a missionary "Messiah complex." This is what the song should be stirring up in each of us who sing and pray with it: it is to invest in the belief that to "rejoice and be glad" is not a childish and naïve notion. It is to acknowledge and embrace with joy that God's *idea*, God's *way*, is the right one, and that surrendering our lives to following Jesus is the only path that can get us there.

I wrote "Blest Are They" thirty-five years ago. But I believe I am called to sing it as a brand new song, as a musical celebration of both downward *mobility* and downward *nobility*. It is a song of rejoicing, but it is also a song of lament that cries out for healing and restoration; ultimately, it is a song of renewed commitment and surrender to Christ. I now feel as though I am singing it again—or perhaps more ardently, it is singing *in* me—as if for the very first time. Join me.

Appendix

Pope Francis & his Six New Beatitudes

Pope Francis, while in Sweden in 2016, preached a homily where he shared six new "Beatitudes" flowing forth from the Sermon on the Mount from Matthew, but also from his conviction that today we are called "to confront the troubles and anxieties of our age with the spirit and love of Jesus."

"New situations require new energy and a new commitment," he said, and then he offered a new list of Beatitudes for modern Christians:

> Blessed are those who remain faithful
> while enduring evils inflicted on them by others and
> forgive them from their heart.

> Blessed are those who look into the eyes of the
> abandoned and marginalized and show them their
> closeness.

> Blessed are those who see God in every person
> and [who] strive to make others also discover [God].

> Blessed are those who protect and care for our common home.
>
> Blessed are those who renounce their own comfort in order to help others.
>
> Blessed are those who pray and work for full communion between Christians.

"All these are messengers of God's mercy and tenderness," Pope Francis said. "Surely they will receive... their merited reward."

I was in Singapore at the time, and was inspired (hopefully) to compose some new verses for "Blest Are They" based on these new touchstones of wisdom from Pope Francis. Here they are (to be matched with the melody of the verses):

> Blest are they, the faithful ones, theirs is the mercy of God.
> Blest are they, who show forgiveness, God will fill their hearts!
>
> > Rejoice and be glad!
> > Blessed are you! Holy are you!
> > Rejoice and be glad!
> > Yours is the kingdom of God!
>
> Blest are they who heal the abandoned, they will be close to God's heart.
> Blest are they who bring forth God's presence, the face of God will be known!

Blest are they, who love all God's children, they are the family of God.
Blest are they who call each one "holy," they shall see God!

Blest are they, who care for the earth, they are the light of God.
Blest are they, who lift up the lowly, they are now one with God!

Blest are you, who pray and work for all the people of God.
Rejoice and be glad, for we are one people, the blessed Body of Christ!

In Gratitude

To the author of Matthew's Gospel, especially for Chapters 5-7;

To Dorothy Day, who invited the guests;

To Barbara Colliander, who made it real for me;

To Fr. John Fitzpatrick, Jan Viktora, Fr. Tom Krenik, Rhea Serazzin, and Michael Grimes (may he rest in blessed peace), for encouraging;

To the people of St. Thomas Aquinas, St. Paul Park, Minnesota, and the original members of the *Emmaus Music Ministry*: Kathy, Mindy, Rose Ann, Mary, Barbie, Sue, Michael, Jim, Barbara, John, Jeanne, Colleen, and Barb—the ensemble who sang it first—and *prayed* it first;

To Jim Waldo, who made it better;

To Fr. Michael Joncas, who told me he liked the hemiola and gave birth to the descant;

To Marty Haugen, who produced the original recording;

To Bob Batastini, Michael Cymbala, and everyone at GIA, who published it;

To Joe Camacho and Betsey Beckman, for helping it to dance and find its wings;

To Lori True—for her grace and prayer-filled voice, always making the fifth verse the best verse;

To N.T. Wright, Fr. Richard Rohr, OFM, Fr. John Dear, Nadia Bolz-Weber, Robert Ellsberg, Art Zannoni, and again, Fr. Michael Joncas, for awakening fresh light on the Beatitudes;

To Brother Mickey McGrath, OSFS, for giving it eyes;

To Jim Knipper, for his friendship, patronage, and creating a "home" for me to explore new creativity;

To Fr. James Martin, SJ, for encouraging me to continue and finish;

To all of those who a part of the Franciscan family—in particular, the online communityof the Order of Baptized Franciscans, for surrounding me with the radical message of Francis and Clare;

To Bonnie Faber, for being my friend and "sister" through many of my chapters and journeys throughout the years;

To the Cretin-Derham Hall Taize' Prayer Community in St. Paul, Minnesota; for providing a praying community free of ego and always full of grace;

To my sisters and brothers in music ministry in the Philippines—the members of Hangad, Bukas Palad, and the Ateneo Chamber Singers—for singing the Christ in all things;

To Barb Conley Waldmiller, for her friendship and editing assistance;

To Bill Huebsch, Fr. Ron Rolheiser, OMI; Megan McKenna, Sr. Kathleen Storms, SSND, Fr. Joe Kempf, Sr. Gertrude Foley, SC; Sr. Sue Mosteller, CSJ; Bishop Remi de Roo, Sr. Helen Prejean, CSJ; Fr. Ray East, Fr. George DeCosta, Pearl Gervais, Fr. Peter Damian Massengill, OFM Conv., and Fr. Ray Kemp, for expanding my spiritual universe;

To blessed friends and colleagues: Rob and Mary Glover, Kate Cuddy, Matt Reichert, Alec Harris, Zack Stachowski, Bob Harvey, Mary Werner, Kathy and Glenn Baybayan, Jo Infante, Dan Kantor, Gary Daigle, Rory Cooney, Fr. Ray East, Andrea Goodrich, Dan Schutte, Stephen Pishner, Matt Maus, Stephen Petrunak, Fiona Dyball, Anna Betancourt, Alissa Hetzner, Jeff and Jean Bross Judge, Tom Franzak, Lynne' Gray, Mary Kay Werner, Fr. Bill Taylor, Bro. Dennis Schmitz, SM; Fr. Ricky Manalo, CSP; Chrissy Fritzen, Jes Garceau, Fr. Alapaki Kim, Fr. Jim Bessert, George Miller, Lou Anne Tighe, Lisa Habeck, Rev. Anita Bradshaw, Lisa Cressy, Greg Papesh, Fr. Virgil Funk, Bob Batastini, Kristen Wenzel, Leisa Anslinger, Rev. Dana Fath Strande, Abbie Rivard, the entire Goldenstein family, Tim and Linda Shriver, Joel Loecken, Luke Rosen, Doug and Brenna Starkebaum, Michael and Anne Frawley Mangan, Mary Reimann, Bill Gokelman, Charlene Kellerman, Katie Riley, and Tom Backen, for their friendship, and who along with everyone else named here, are true witnesses and wisdom bearers; for being the ongoing "Sermon on the Mount People" in my life;

To Helen and to Jeffrey, Colleen, and Mary, for their love and steadfast presence;

To the memory of Sue Seid-Martin, who smiled, and who I believe still is;

To the memory of Roberta Kolasa, SJ, for always believing;

To the memory of my Father, for arms always outstretched;

To the memory of my Mother, for always being delighted;

And to all who keep singing and living the Sermon;

Blessed are you. **DH**

Acknowledgements

Most of the music cited below is available on the companion CD for this book, *Rejoice and Be Glad: (Y)Ours is the Kingdom of God* produced by GIA Publications, Inc., (CD-1058)

> GIA Publications, Inc.
> 7404 South Mason Avenue
> Chicago, IL 60638 (www.giamusic.com)

The text for "Blest are They" by David Haas. Copyright © 1985 GIA Publications, Inc. Reprinted with permission. All rights reserved.

The text for "In the Power of Christ" by David Haas. Copyright © 2003 GIA Publications. Inc. Reprinted with permission. All rights reserved.

The text for "Every Moment" by David Haas. Copyright © 2015 GIA Publications, Inc. Reprinted with permission. All rights reserved.

The text for "I Will Walk with You" by David Haas. Copyright © 2018 GIA Publications, Inc. Reprinted with permission. All rights reserved.

The text for "Baptized in Water" by John Bell. Copyright © 2008, WGRG, Iona Community, Scotland. GIA Publications, Inc., exclusive North American Agent. Reprinted with permission. All rights reserved.

The text for "Goodness is Stronger than Evil" by Desmond Tutu, adapt. by John Bell. Copyright © 1996, WGRG, Iona Community, Scotland. GIA